Pebble®
Bilingüe/ Bilingual Plus

Datos geniales sobre deportes/
Cool Sports Facts

Datos geniales sobre básquetbol

Cool Basketball Facts

WITHDRAWN

por/by Abby Czeskleba

Editora consultora/Consulting Editor:

Gail Saunders-Smith, PhD

Consultor/Consultant: Craig Coenen, PhD
Profesor Adjunto de Historia/Associate Professor of History
Mercer County Community College
West Windsor, New Jersey

CAPSTONE PRESS
a capstone imprint

Pebble Plus is published by Capstone Press,
1710 Roe Crest Drive, North Mankato, Minnesota 56003.
www.capstonepub.com

Library of Congress Cataloging-in-Publication Data
Czeskleba, Abby.
[Cool basketball facts. Spanish.]
Datos geniales sobre básquetbol = Cool basketball facts / by Abby Czeskleba.
p. cm. — (Pebble plus bilingue/bilingual)
Includes index.
ISBN 978-1-4296-9215-1 (library binding)
ISBN 978-1-62065-336-4 (ebook PDF)
1. Basketball—Miscellanea—Juvenile literature. I. Title.
GV885.1.C94 2013
796.323—dc23   2011050103

Summary: Simple text and full-color photos illustrate facts about the rules, equipment, and records of basketball.

Editorial Credits
Erika L. Shores, editor; Strictly Spanish, translation services; Kyle Grenz, designer; Eric Manske, bilingual book designer
    and production specialist; Eric Gohl, media researcher

Photo Credits
Comstock Images, cover (basketball), back cover, 1
Dreamstime/Mike Liu, cover
NBAE via Getty Images Inc./David Liam Kyle, 5; Dick Raphael, 7; Jesse D. Garrabrant, 13, 21; Lisa Blumenfeld, 15;
    Melissa Majchrzak, 11; Nathaniel S. Butler, 19; Noah Graham, 17
Newscom/Icon SMI/Albert Pena, 9

Note to Parents and Teachers

The Datos geniales sobre deportes/Cool Sports Facts series supports national social studies
standards related to people, places, and culture. This book describes and illustrates basketball.
The images support early readers in understanding the text. The repetition of words and
phrases helps early readers learn new words. This book also introduces early readers to subject-
specific vocabulary words, which are defined in the Glossary section. Early readers may need
assistance to read some words and to use the Table of Contents, Glossary, Internet Sites, and
Index sections of the book.

Printed in the United States of America in North Mankato, Minnesota.
042012   006682CGF12

Table of Contents

Tabla de contenidos

Slam Dunk!

Each year, NBA players
slam dunk in front of
21 million fans.
In 2009, players dunked
more than 9,000 times.

¡Clavada!

Cada año, los jugadores de la
NBA hacen clavadas frente a
21 millones de aficionados.
En 2009, los jugadores hicieron
clavadas más de 9,000 veces.

NBA stands for National Basketball Association.

NBA son las siglas en inglés de la Asociación Nacional de Básquetbol.

Cool Equipment

In 1985, Michael Jordan wore different shoes than his teammates. He broke NBA rules. The NBA fined him $5,000 for each game.

Equipo genial

En 1985, Michael Jordan usó zapatos diferentes a los de sus compañeros de equipo. Rompió las reglas de la NBA. La NBA lo multó con $5,000 dólares por partido.

Michael Jordan

Teams get six basketballs
to use during warm-ups
before a game.
The number of balls is listed
in the NBA rule book.

Los equipos tienen seis balones de
básquetbol para usar durante el
calentamiento antes de un partido.
El número de balones está indicado
en el libro de reglamento de la NBA.

Cool Rules

A team with the basketball
has 24 seconds to take a shot.
A player must shoot a free
throw within 10 seconds.

Reglas geniales

El equipo que tiene el balón de
básquetbol tiene 24 segundos
para hacer un tiro.
Un jugador debe hacer un tiro libre en
menos de 10 segundos.

shot clock

cronómetro
de tiros

11

It's against the rules
to kick the ball on purpose.
Kicking the ball into the stands
gets the player kicked out
of the game.

Es contra las reglas patear
el balón a propósito.
Patear el balón hacia las gradas
hace que el jugador sea
expulsado del juego.

Cool Records

The Women's National Basketball
Association began in 1997.
Lisa Leslie scored the first dunk
in the WNBA.

Reglas geniales

La Asociación Nacional de Básquetbol
Femenino empezó en 1997.
Lisa Leslie anotó la primera clavada
en la WNBA.

In 2008, Jordan Farmar set
a dribbling record.
At the NBA All-Star Jam Session,
Farmar dribbled a ball
228 times in one minute.

En 2008, Jordan Farmar impuso un
récord de dribleo.
En la Sesión de Juego de Estrellas
de la NBA, Farmar dribló el balón
228 veces en un minuto.

NBA star Robert Parish played in
1,611 NBA games.
No one has played more
NBA games than he has.

Robert Parish, estrella de la NBA,
jugó en 1,611 partidos de la NBA.
Nadie ha jugado en más partidos en
la NBA que él.

The Boston Celtics have won the most NBA championships with 17. They won 11 of these championships in just 13 years.

Los Celtics de Boston han ganado la mayoría de los campeonatos de la NBA con un total de 17. Ganaron 11 de estos campeonatos en apenas 13 años.

21

Glossary

dribble—to bounce a basketball off the floor using one hand

dunk—when a player jumps and slams the ball down into the basket from above the rim

fine—to charge someone money for breaking a rule

free throw—a shot taken from the free-throw line by a player when the other team makes a foul

Internet Sites

FactHound offers a safe, fun way to find Internet sites related to this book. All of the sites on FactHound have been researched by our staff.

Here's all you do:

Visit *www.facthound.com*

Type in this code: 9781429692151

Super-cool stuff! Check out projects, games and lots more at **www.capstonekids.com**

Glosario

la clavada—cuando un jugador salta y coloca con toda fuerza el balón dentro de la red desde arriba del aro

driblar—botar un balón de básquetbol en el suelo usando una mano

la multa—cobrar dinero a alguien por romper una regla

el tiro libre—un tiro que lanza un jugador desde la línea de tiro libre cuando el otro equipo comete una falta

Sitios de Internet

FactHound brinda una forma segura y divertida de encontrar sitios de Internet relacionados con este libro. Todos los sitios en FactHound han sido investigados por nuestro personal.

Esto es todo lo que tienes que hacer:

Visita *www.facthound.com*

Ingresa este código: 9781429692151

¡Algo súper divertido! Hay proyectos, juegos y mucho más en www.capstonekids.com

Index

Índice